�

Heaven Sense

Other books by J. P. Arendzen
from Sophia Institute Press®:

Ten Minutes a Day to Heaven

Understanding the Trinity

J. P. Arendzen

Heaven Sense

What Scripture and the Catholic Church Really Teach about Heaven

SOPHIA INSTITUTE PRESS®
Manchester, New Hampshire

Sophia Institute Press®
Box 5284, Manchester, NH 03108
1-800-888-9344
www.sophiainstitute.com

Nihil obstat: Arthur J. Scanlan, S.T.D., *Censor Librorum*
Imprimatur: Patrick Cardinal Hayes, Archbishop of New York

Library of Congress Cataloging-in-Publication Data

Arendzen, J. P. (John Peter), b. 1873-
    [Church triumphant]
    Heaven sense : what scripture and the Catholic Church really teach about heaven / J.P. Arendzen.
        p. cm.
    Originally published: The Church triumphant. New York : Macmillan, 1928.
    Includes bibliographical references.
    ISBN 1-928832-16-4 (pbk. : alk. paper)
    1. Heaven — Christianity. 2. Catholic Church — Doctrines. I. Title.
BT846.3.A74 2004
236′.4 — dc22   2004023386

04 05 06 07 08 09 10 9 8 7 6 5 4 3 2 1

✻

Contents

✻

⁎

Foreword

Perhaps the topic that the priest finds most difficult of pulpit treatment is Heaven. This is not due to any dearth of theological or devotional matter on the subject. The difficulty arises, in the first place, from the fact that it requires far more than ordinary ability to visualize the happiness of Heaven as a compelling motive of right conduct, without running the risk of using comparisons between sensual and spiritual joys which are not only unbecoming, but sometimes ridiculous. Again, it is nearly impossible to give anything approaching a popular exposition of the essential happiness of the Beatific Vision.

Within the narrow limits of this small volume, Fr. Arendzen succeeds admirably in setting forth the Catholic doctrine of Heaven in a fashion that will prove helpful to the priest and the layman. Avoiding anything that approximates the descriptive treatment of Heaven, which mars so much of our devotional literature, and rigidly confining himself to the strict letter of Faith and its theological conclusions, he presents the story of the Church Triumphant as a reasonable and attractive doctrine.

In the introduction, Fr. Arendzen shows Heaven as the consummation of the Church of God begun in Eden and continued in time. Hell, the opposite of Heaven, is shown to be a frustration of God's purpose in His providence over man and man's complete defeat; the happiness of Heaven is found in the vision of God Himself as the only divine revelation that fully satisfies our mental and moral faculties. By way of secondary sources of heavenly happiness, we have communion with Christ in His human nature, with our Lady, the angels and the saints. Supplementing these sources, we have what might be called the human relationships in Heaven of one soul with another.

Too much thought, as a rule, is given, both in public preachments and private meditations, to Hell, and not nearly enough to Heaven. No one spoke more earnestly than our Lord about the condign punishment that is the natural consequence of deliberate and continued sin. It should not be forgotten, however, that His promise of God's own immediate companionship with those who love Him in both this life and the next is very frequently stressed in the New Testament.

There is undoubtedly a distinct place in our Catholic English literature for this book.

Rev. Harold Purcell, C.P.

Editor's note: The biblical quotations in the following pages are taken from the Douay-Rheims edition of the Old and New Testaments. Where applicable, quotations have been cross-referenced with the differing names and enumeration in the Revised Standard Version, using the following symbol: (RSV =).

ჟ

Introduction

For God, the creation and the final consummation of all things are ever present to His eternity. For men, who exist in time, their creation and their consummation are separated by the slow sequence of change measured by many days, many years, and many ages. God created us by an act of thought; He willed, He spoke, and we were. We *are*, because He knows us. On the impossible supposition that we should ever pass out of His sight, we would instantaneously cease to be and would sink back into the nothing from which we came.

Our creation meant that we entered into the sight of God, and our continued existence means that He keeps us in sight; our very being depends on His mind. Our consummation will be when we know God even as we are known, when we see Him, who has ever seen us and whose sight is our life. God knew us in order that one day we might know Him; such is the *alpha* and *omega*, the beginning and end of all human history.

The Church of God, in the full sense of the word, is the multitude of those whom God has called to eternal life.

"We know," said St. Paul, "that unto those who love God all things cooperate unto good even unto those who according to His purpose are called to be saints. For those whom He foreknew, He also predestined to become likened unto the image of His Son, that He might be the firstborn among many brethren. But those whom He predestined, He also justified, but those whom He justified He also glorified."[1]

In this sense, there is but one Church of God from the days of Adam and Eve until the day when the whole multitude of the saved will be glorified around the throne of God. The Church of God began in Paradise and continues in Heaven.

On earth, it is divided into the church of the primitive covenant, that of the Mosaic, and that of the New or Christian covenant, but these three divisions can be

[1] Cf. Rom. 8:28-30.

united under the one name of Church Militant, for man's life on earth is a warfare, as Scripture says.[2] To this warfare there is only one final alternative: either Heaven or Hell.

Hell is complete defeat and everlasting loss. Those who enter Hell completely pass out of the Communion of Saints and the Church of the Redeemed; they are outside the bond of charity and the benefit of the Atonement of Christ.

Those who enter Purgatory not only remain within the Church and the Communion of Saints, but are its holy and privileged members, who have made their salvation sure. Their state, however, is not a permanent one, and while it lasts, it combines the joys of security and the calm of resignation with the most intense pain of being deprived of the sight of God. Hence, the multitude of those waiting souls is called the Church Suffering.

Heaven is the only decisive and ultimate victory of which man is capable. Hence, the company of those who have fought the good fight, won the battle, and entered into the land of their conquest is called the Church Triumphant.

[2] Job 7:1.

We shall study the nature of that ultimate triumph, that celestial consummation which awaits those who persevered unto the end and have received from the eternal King the reward that never passes away. In Heaven, man will achieve the perfection of his manhood in the supernatural order as God intended it. This will mean the complete satisfaction of his faculties of mind and will by the sight and possession of God Himself; it will mean the glorification also of his body and its faculties, because the body will be the handmaid of his soul in the perfection of his celestial life.

We must therefore consider his heavenly happiness first in regard to his mind, then in regard to his will, and finally in regard to his body. We shall conclude by considering some of the consequences and implications of his eternal bliss, and by studying some special questions concerning Heaven.

Heaven Sense

How will I see God in Heaven?

Heaven is essentially the sight of God face-to-face.

Almost eighteen hundred years ago St. Irenaeus wrote:

> The things that are impossible with men are possible with God. For man indeed of himself does not see God. But God of His own will is seen by those whom He wills, when He wills, and as He wills. For God is mighty in all. He was seen then [by the Prophets in the Old Testament] through the Spirit of prophecy; He is now seen in the New Covenant, by adoption also, through the Son; but in the kingdom of Heaven, He will be seen even as Father. Man will be prepared by the Spirit in the Son of God. Man will be brought to the Father by the Son; man will be endowed with incorruption by the

Father unto everlasting life, which comes to everyone by the fact of his seeing God. For as those who see the light are in the light and perceive its brightness; thus also those who see God are in God, perceiving His brightness. This brightness gives them their life; hence, they who see God, see life. God is beyond created grasp, intelligence, and sight, but He will put Himself within human sight, intelligence, and grasp for the purpose of giving life to those who perceive and see Him. God's greatness is indeed unsearchable, but so also is His loving kindness unutterable, even that loving kindness by which, being seen, He gives life to those who see Him.[3]

At first, it may seem difficult to realize that our happiness in Heaven can possibly consist in an act of contemplation and love. On earth, the common idea of enjoying oneself consists in some gratification of the senses: a sumptuous banquet, sweet music, healthy exercise, a beautiful landscape; or the company and praise of our fellowmen,

---

[3] St. Ireneaus (c. 125-c. 203; student of St. Polycarp, missionary, bishop of Lyons, and Church Father), *Adv. Haeres*, IV, 20, 5.

the achievement of some great work through the exercise of our brain and skill, the discovery of something fresh and new, the traveling through unknown and sunlit lands. These and a thousand other things flit before the human mind when it imagines supreme happiness, for this happiness is thought of as an endless variety of such things as our own experience on earth suggests. A life of contemplation may seem a pale and attenuated existence, holding little attraction for us. On reflection, however, it becomes more and more evident that the highest and happiest life must be the complete satisfaction of mind and will in the sight and possession of an infinite personal Being.

Even on this earth, the greatest known joy is intimacy — that is, knowledge and nearness with another intelligent being. Imagine a mother, after the Great War, gazing again on the face of her son, and hearing his voice, and then clasping him in her embrace, and holding him as her very own possession, of which the battlefield had almost robbed her! The first moments of their mutual happiness contain a joy so intense that all other so-called enjoyments are as nothing in comparison.

Or imagine a husband and a wife who have been parted by strange misfortunes, and after years of separation meet again. As a matter of fact, this theme has ever been elaborated in all human literature, and we may rest assured that it will remain so as long as man lives here below.

No doubt this theme of storytellers, poets, and songsters has been degraded times out of number because of the carnal and sexual element that so often is intruded, or rather, intrudes itself. But nobler minds, at least, can realize that the sensual side of this earthly affection ought not and need not be the dominant factor in true human love, that the knowledge and spiritual possession of one another can be the source of a quasi-delirium of pure joy even on earth.

True, this does not often last long, but at least as long as it lasts, it is supposed to outweigh all other things. Pain, poverty, and distress only provoke a smile, and the very comparison of such joy with other earthly goods is disclaimed as a degradation. "Strong as death is love, and many waters cannot quench its fire."[4] Given the infinity of God, God must be infinitely beautiful and infinitely lovable. So, far from a pale and extenuated existence, Heaven is the romance, the never-ending love story of the soul and God.

---

[4] Cf. Cant. 8:6-7 (RSV = Song of Sol. 8:6-7).

How will I see God in Heaven?

ॐ

Will I actually see God?

Holy Scripture certainly makes it perfectly plain that our eternal happiness will consist in seeing God.

> We know in part; and we prophesy in part. But when that which is perfect is come, that which is in part shall be done away. When I was a child, I spoke as a child, I understood as a child, I thought as a child. But when I became a man, I put away the things of a child. We see now through a glass in a dark manner; but then face-to-face. Now I know in part; but then I shall know even as I am known.[5]

> We are now the sons of God; and it hath not yet appeared what we shall be. We know that when He shall appear, we shall be like to Him, because we shall see Him as He is.[6]

> Father, I will that where I am, they also whom Thou hast given me may be with me, that they may

[5] 1 Cor. 13:9-12.
[6] 1 John 3:2.

see my glory which Thou hast given me, because Thou hast loved me before the creation of the world.[7]

Despise no one of these little ones; for I say to you that their angels in Heaven always see the face of my Father who is in Heaven.[8]

In the midst . . . was the tree of life. . . . The throne of God and of the Lamb shall be in it. And His servants shall serve Him. And they shall see His face, and His name shall be on their foreheads. And night shall be no more. And they shall not need the light of the lamp, nor the light of the sun, because the Lord God shall enlighten them. And they shall reign forever and ever.[9]

Some people speak as if the sight of God after death were the natural reward for those who have led good lives. This is a great mistake. It is not natural to any created being, however good, to see God. God is infinite; a created being is finite, limited, circumscribed, and it is not natural

[7] John 17:24.
[8] Matt. 18:10.
[9] Apoc. 22:2-5 (RSV = Rev. 22:2-5).

for the finite to perceive the infinite. Not that the infinite merely exceeds the finite in extent, and that therefore the finite could see only a part or a portion of it. The infinite has no parts. The infinite cannot be divided. One cannot see half of it, or a third, or a tenth; one either sees it as a unity in its entirety, or one does not see it at all.

The infinite exceeds the finite not in extent, but in innermost being. God does not belong to the same category of being as the creature; in fact, He does not belong to any category of being at all: He is unique. There is nothing with which to compare Him. He stands utterly by Himself. His essence, His life infinitely exceed ours. Hence, it cannot be natural for any creature to see God — that is, to know Him as He is. We are indeed like God, but not as one human being is like another. We are like Him, as the image in a mirror is like the man who stands in front of it. God is the reality, we the image. Created reality consists in this very imagehood, and is of necessity infinitely distant from the self-subsistent infinite reality that is its Creator. So far is it from being natural for a created being to understand, to grasp God, to see Him face-to-face, to know Him in the way in which He knows Himself, that the human mind could never have known, but for divine revelation, that such vision was possible.

Even after divine revelation, the human mind cannot understand how it is, although it humbly believes God's word. The "how" of it — I mean the core of this mystery of the Beatific Vision — completely escapes us; it remains as utter a secret as the blessed Trinity, or the Incarnation, or the blessed Sacrament. The Beatific Vision is the crowning mystery of Christianity, a mystery that leaves the human mind aghast and is acceptable only by the power of faith. The Beatific Vision is a free gift of God to man exceeding all natural merit of virtue by an absolute measure, and not only the merit of human virtue, but that of any angels and archangels, cherubim or seraphim; nay, even of Mary the Mother of God. God, infinite though He be, could not, even by an exercise of His absolute omnipotence, create a being to whom it should be *natural* to enjoy the Beatific Vision.

༈

Will I see God as I see things on earth?

Let us study the workings of our mind a little.

Here on earth, we have only one definite mode according to which we know things. By our five senses we come in touch with the outer world, and through them we form sense-images. These sense-images we have in common with the animal world, but, being men, and not animals only, by the action of our spiritual soul or mind we abstract the essence of things from them — that is, we regard not merely *this* tree, *this* house, *this* dog, or *this* man, but transcending their concrete individuality we refer to a tree, a house, a dog, a man, abstracting completely from all those special characteristics by which they are constituted as concrete units; in other words, we form their concept, or general idea. Moreover, we can conceive their abstract relations; we conceive length and breadth and height and measure, and we compare them.

Nay, we ascend to such high abstractions as right or wrong, virtue or vice, holiness or sin. Then we can combine our many ideas into judgments, and chain these together into arguments, and reason from truth to truth.

In this way we come to the supreme conclusion that God *is*, that some infinite, eternal, self-existent cause must have made this world, and thus in a supereminent way contain within Himself all the highest perfections of the world He has made. During this life, we have no other means of knowledge, no other means of access to reality except the way we have thus described. It is an indirect and discursive way, incapable of leading us to God directly, incapable of bringing us to God as He is in Himself.

Now, after death, even though our body is separated from our soul, our mind does not change its nature. Some are under the impression that death acts like magic and changes our innermost being; but this is not so. If God did not intervene, if God left nature merely to itself, the human mind would possess no further knowledge beyond what it had gained by inference and reasoning. It would know God in an abstract and merely analogous way; it would never know God directly and immediately — never by sight. It might still have been rewarded by some happy life in reward for its virtue; this life would have been endless, but it would not have been the Beatific Vision. There would have been a quasi-infinite difference between that state and the blissful direct sight of God.

What, then, will this vision be? It will be a vision without any sense or any thought-images. Obviously no sense-image can intervene, for God is in no sense corporeal. Moreover, there will be no thought-image or idea. What do we mean by this? The mind will not form an abstract representation or idea of God; it will have no "mental picture," as it has in the case of all other things here on earth. The sense-image on the brain is grasped by the mind. It sinks into the mind; the mind grips it and holds it and transforms itself accordingly: it conceives it, as we say. A thought is a concept, a mental impression, by means of which the thing that is without us is seen by the mind. It is, as it were, a lens between our mental eye and the reality. We know a thing by the idea we form of it; without such ideal medium, our mind knows nothing.

Or perhaps, instead of the comparison of a lens, it may be better to use that of a seal imprinted upon wax. The schoolmen speak of a *species impressa* and a *species expressa*. Every act of thought modifies the mind. It is as if external reality impressed itself on the mind and shaped and molded it. There is, however, this difference: the mental die forces itself upon the wax and causes its conformity with the engraving on its surface. In thinking, it is the mind which is the active principle and which holds and conforms itself to the external reality and absorbs it, in a sense, by taking it unto itself. Now, a created thing is understood by us precisely because we thus mentally grasp its outlines, those limitations of a being which make it that being and not another. It is clear that God cannot be understood in this way, because God is essentially infinite and has no limitations. No idea, since it is necessarily limited, can adequately represent the infinite God.

It remains, therefore, that God should, in some mysterious way, fulfill the role that, in our natural cognitive processes, is played by the "idea." God will render Himself immediately present and intelligible to our minds.

In this way we have never as yet known anything on earth. All things remain, as it were, outside us; they enter into our minds only by way of an "idea." God will not remain outside us. He will be within our mind itself, and there we shall see Him. The nearest approximation to such knowledge on earth is our knowledge of ourselves. We know ourselves because we are ourselves; we are present to ourselves in our innermost being. Hence, Holy Scripture uses this knowledge as a means of comparison: "Then I shall know even as I am known."

We must not, therefore, imagine God in the Beatific Vision as some outside object to look at, but as dwelling within the very essence of our soul, and thus being perceived from within by direct contact. Of course, even of our earthly life it is true that "in Him we live, we move, we have our being."[10]

God not only created us in the past, but maintains us in being in the present; our whole being continually rests upon Him. We exist only because He incessantly inwardly sustains us.

[10] Cf. Acts 17:28.

We are kept in being by God as the image in the mirror is kept in being by the person continuing to stand in front of it. Our innermost self is in God and by God, but we do not realize it. We do not perceive God. Our being is in contact with Him, but not our knowledge; when our knowledge also attains Him directly, then we shall possess the Beatific Vision.

The principle that rules all intelligence and understanding is that we can know things only in the measure in which we are similar to them. A thing that has nothing in common with us, we could never understand, but inasmuch as we resemble them can we grasp them with our mind. So is it also with regard to our understanding God. We shall know Him, and therefore, says the Scripture, "We shall be like unto Him." Our life shall be in conscious contact with His, and His life shall, as it were, overflow into ours and pervade us through and through, and thus we shall know Him.

A humble comparison may help us: throw a bar of iron into a blazing furnace and leave it there until it is molten metal in the midst of the fire, and the eye can no longer see the iron. As that iron knows the fire, so shall we know God. Our innermost being will thrill and throb in unison with God's life, and we shall be fully conscious of it. True, by grace we are on earth already "sharers of the divine nature,"[11] as St Peter tells us, but the effect of that participation of divine life is in some sense suspended, because our soul is still in our mortal body. Its mode of knowledge is restricted and restrained by our earthly conditions. Set it free from this mortal body, and grace changes into glory; the soul enters into its supernatural birthright.

God, in order to make this apprehension possible, creates in us a new faculty, which we call by the technical name of *lumen gloriae*, "the light of glory." By this, our cognitive faculty is raised to a supernatural state, being thus enabled to perform an act that exceeds not only the normal human mode and measure of knowing, but the mode and measure of any creature whatever.

❧

Will I see all three
Persons of the Trinity?

But here we are faced with the difficulty that the finite can never grasp the infinite. The difficulty would be insuperable if the Beatific Vision involved that the human mind encompassed God with its knowledge. This indeed

[11] Cf. 2 Pet. 1:4.

would be impossible. The blessed will see the whole of God — for God has no parts — yet they will not exhaust His infinite intelligibility. God alone can know Himself as fully as He can be known.

As in Heaven faith and hope cease and only charity remains, the blessed in Heaven will cease to *believe* in the blessed Trinity; they will cease to accept it on faith, for faith will be replaced by vision. The great mystery will be mystery no longer, for they will see the Father, the Son, and the Holy Spirit face-to-face.

The blessed contemplate not merely the divine nature as such, by a mental abstraction distinguishing it from the threefold personality as we do on earth; they see God as He is, and therefore they see the Three Persons in the Trinity. Their understanding of the mystery will, of course, not be infinite and comprehensive; it will be only finite apprehension, the intensity and depth of which varies with the measure of the *lumen gloriae* they receive. Their understanding of it will be nonetheless direct and intuitive, thus completely satiating their intelligence, so that all further searching into the truth as into a mystery will entirely cease.

Thus will be fulfilled Christ's words: "No one knows the Father except the Son and he to whom the Son wills to reveal Him."[12] The blessed know the Father through the Son in the Holy Spirit. They see the Unbegotten Source of the Godhead, who is the Father, through the Son, whom He eternally begets. They perceive Him through His Word and Utterance, through Him who is "the splendor of His glory and the figure of His substance."[13] They see both Father and Son in the Holy Spirit, who dwells within them, and in whose light they participate through the light of glory.

The blessed are adopted sons of God, brothers and co-heirs of Christ, and will therefore rejoice in eternity in love and worship of the Second Person of the Trinity as united to them in a brotherhood through grace and glory. They rejoice in the indwelling of the Holy Spirit, whose temple they are. They rejoice in the adoration of the First Person, from whom all good things flow and to whom they have learned from Christ to say, "Abba, Father."

As by Baptism they were baptized in the name of the Father and of the Son and of the Holy Spirit when first they received the gift of sanctifying grace, so when grace is changed into glory, they will be hallowed and sanctified

[12] Cf. Matt. 11:27.
[13] Cf. Heb. 1:3.

in that Name. Their heavenly life will be one continual Glory Be.

In the souls of the just on earth, the three divine Persons dwelt, according to the promise of Christ: "If any man love me . . . we will come to him and will make our abode with him."[14] Of this indwelling, however, the just on earth are not normally conscious. In heavenly glory, this indwelling will be consciously perceived and enjoyed by the blessed. In consequence, the blessed stand in a threefold conscious relation to God, whom they contemplate and possess within themselves. When they re-echo the threefold "Holy, holy, holy" of the Cherubim, they will understand the full meaning of the Trisagion and ascribe this triple song of praise by love and adoration to the triune God within them whose unveiled presence they hold and embrace.

[14] John 14:23.

Chapter Two

⚜

How will I love God in Heaven?

Although we describe our eternal reward as "blissful sight," this description does not exhaust the reality; it is not, as it were, a definition, a complete designation of it. Even in eternity we shall have not merely mind, but also will. Not only our intelligence, but our human desire will be totally satiated, for in knowing Him who is the fount of all truth, we shall possess Him who is the Infinite Good. As God is infinite, He can belong to endlessly many creatures, but still be to each of them totally his. "I am thy reward exceeding great,"[15] said God to Abraham; but this saying in strictest truth is applicable to each one of the blessed.

Seeing God and possessing God are in a sense the same thing, or, rather, they are the obverse and reverse of a

---

[15] Gen. 15:1.

medal. To see is to enjoy; to enjoy is to possess. God is infinite beauty, but to embrace infinite beauty by knowledge is to possess it. God will give Himself to us. A friend gives himself to a friend by throwing himself into his friend's arms and being pressed to his bosom. A spirit embraces not with material fleshly arms, but by the power of thought. We shall clasp God to our bosom spiritually, and we shall be united to Him with closer bonds than ever a beloved was joined to a lover.

These are not mere expressions of poetic exaggeration or mere emotional piety. They are endorsed by strict philosophy and theology; they are almost technical in their value. To possess God is supreme happiness, for God is infinite beauty and lovableness.

If a man wishes to call his imagination to aid — and it is not unlawful in this matter — he should recall the greatest and grandest scene of beauty he has ever gazed upon, the most entrancing melody he ever heard, and remember that God created nature, and that nature is a feeble reflection of God. He should think of the person he most dearly loves or loved on earth, the dearest face, the tenderest heart he knows of, and then say to himself that all human goodness, the sum of all human lovableness is as a drop in the ocean of God's love and magnificence.

A further thought that will aid us is that the love between God and ourselves will be mutual. God is not merely
a picture to be looked at, a scene to be contemplated.
God is personal, and He returns the gaze we cast upon
Him. God is a living God, not a mere effulgence of imper-
sonal glory, however great. Our soul will be joined to God
in mutual affection; He will ever whisper in our ears: "I
have chosen you," and we shall answer, however humbly,
"And I have chosen You." Our union in Heaven is the
outcome of our free deliberate acts on earth, continued in
eternity.

These transports, of course, will be mental, spiritual,
without any physical emotion, and without that exhaus-
tion which on earth follows the outpouring of mere natural human affections; but they will on that account be
only the more intense. When, after the resurrection, we
shall possess our bodies again, even our glorified flesh will
no doubt share in the exaltation of our spirit, and experience a sweetness indescribable to us now, but correspond-
ing to our state of soul, and unaccompanied by that
fatigue which is caused by continued emotion here.

All love is essentially an act that goes out from one
being to another. It is the precise opposite of selfishness or
self-centeredness. It is benevolence toward another; it is

complacency in the good of another; it is return of affection for a good received from another. All love is union of some kind, but union is impossible unless there are at least two parties, and each of these communicates with the other, or gives itself (or at least something of itself) to the other. The more perfect the love, the more complete the surrender of the lover to the loved. In consequence, the love by which the blessed love God is one of supreme altruism. On earth, we often say that the more a man goes out of himself, the more he leaves himself behind and forgets himself, the more perfect is his love. This is true in the highest manner of the love of the blessed in Heaven.

⚜

Will I forget myself in Heaven?

It is sometimes objected that the Christian conception of an eternal reward in Heaven is a selfish ideal. This objection rests on a complete misunderstanding. The blessed in Heaven are indeed supremely happy. But this happiness is the necessary consequence of their love of God. They are happy, not in loving themselves, but in loving God. Heaven is the highest act of self-surrender of which a creature is capable. Each one of the blessed is eternally conscious that he belongs to another, and this very consciousness is the source of his happiness. Heaven is the absolute cessation of self-love, if by *self* we understand something separate and independent of God.

Do the blessed, then, "forget" themselves in God? Have the blessed no love for themselves? Of course they do. The blessed know that they are themselves the objects of divine love, and in loving God, they love all that God loves, including themselves. The precise reason the blessed love themselves lies in that they are conscious of being the objects of God's love. They know themselves as the image and likeness of God, and they see in themselves a partial mirroring of the infinite perfection of God. They love God in themselves, for whatever perfection or excellence they possess is a gift of God, and the effect of His creative will. They love it because it is His work. They love themselves because they are His.

Heaven is no home for mock humility. St. Paul wrote, "By the grace of God I am what I am, and the grace of God in me has not been void."[16] So the blessed say, "By the glory of God I am what I am, and the glory of God in me is not void." This is not in discord with their former song

[16] 1 Cor. 15:10.

on earth: "To the King, immortal and invisible, to God alone be honor and glory throughout the ages of ages."[17] The only difference is that the King once invisible is now seen face-to-face. To Him alone indeed be glory, for our glory is His.

Imagine that a sculptor could make statues, not of dead marble, but endowed with life and thought. Imagine, further, that the life and thought of these statues remained continually dependent on the active will of the sculptor who first fashioned them. Imagine, thirdly, that each of these statues was a self-portrait of the sculptor, portraying him in different attitudes and with different charms. Imagine, lastly, that these living statues knew and loved the sculptor who made them and keeps them in being. You will have then imagined something resembling the blessed in Heaven. The more these living statues loved the sculptor, the more they would love themselves as portraying one or other of his perfections.

The blessed love themselves, but their love does not rest ultimately there, but in God, whom *alone* they love for Himself. Their self-love is but an aspect of their love for God. A very telling, although imperfect, parallel of

[17] Cf. 1 Tim. 1:17.

this celestial love is sometimes found in the utterance of lover to beloved: "The only reason I care for myself is that you love me."

⚜

Will I have any desires in Heaven?

The sight and love of God will constitute the complete satisfaction of all our desires. During our mortal life, we are beings in progress, in process of evolution toward our final state. The Beatific Vision is that final state. Our mortal life is a tending toward the perfection of our being.

We Catholics are, as a matter of fact, great believers in evolution, but we do not trouble ourselves so much about the evolution of the past, for, whatever it has been, it has only historical interest; we cannot change it now. What has been, has been. We believe in the only evolution that really matters, the evolution we are actually undergoing, and in which our own free will plays a part. Because on this earth we are evolving beings, evolving according to God's supernatural plan toward a life in union with Him, our mortal life is essentially imperfect.

Because we are imperfect, our life here is one of longing, seeking, hoping for the future. All this will one day end. We shall not always be dissatisfied with what we have and are. Our eternal existence will not be one of endless craving and not yet possessing, a waiting for something beyond; the fullness of our being will come at last, and our life will be one of tranquil possession. That sacred restlessness which necessarily marks even the holiest life on earth, precisely because it has not reached the term and purpose of its existence, will pass away.

We cannot picture to ourselves a life without some unfulfilled desires, yet reason tells us that, in the consummation of all things, unfulfilled desires are an impossibility for those who have received their reward exceedingly great, in the possession of God. Their whole being is satiated. The question "Do you lack anything? Is there still anything you need?" would, if put to the lowliest of the saints, provoke a smile and the answer, "How could I, since I have God?"

In Heaven, we are at the end of life's journey; we are in God's Paradise; we need not, indeed we cannot, travel beyond. Heaven, therefore, is in a sense something stationary, since it is the complete fulfillment of our being. We have reached God, and we can reach no further. Striving is over; there is now only the unchangeable joy of possession, of repose in God. It is, indeed, the "eternal rest" we so often pray that God may give to the souls in Purgatory.

Is there activity in Heaven?

Yet this complete repose and satisfaction of our being is no mere passive state. It is the most intense activity. God Himself, as we know, is called in Catholic philosophy "pure activity," and in the measure in which we approach God, the intensity of our life increases. Heaven is all activity.

The love of the blessed is always active. On earth, our acts of love toward our neighbor last for a while: they last while we think of them; they cease when the necessities of our daily life force us to think of something else. Even our love of God that we exercise on earth is manifested by intermittent acts. Great saints may, indeed, in their waking moments, make an almost continuous act of the love of God, but even they must occasionally interrupt their communion with God to attend to other things.

In Heaven, as the Beatific Vision is but one unceasing act, so likewise the act of love is one single uninterrupted act that lasts throughout eternity. This act of blissful love not only never ceases, but it never varies, whether in intensity or in the object to which it is directed; for the soul's power of loving is unchangeable and always exercised to the utmost, and God, the object loved, is always clearly seen in all His lovableness as far as the particular soul can apprehend it.

On earth, we can exercise our love for God on different grounds, loving Him now for His justice, now for His mercy, now for His wisdom, now for His tenderness. In Heaven, we shall see that all God's attributes are identical with His being. This one act of supernatural human love will contain within itself all aspects of love: love of benevolence, love of complacency, love of gratitude — that is, the will that God should be what He is, the Infinite Good, a pure delight begotten of the contemplation of His infinite goodness, and a realization that our share in His happiness is due to His generous bounty.

Shall we never tire of the very intensity of our love toward God? Will the transports of joy and love never create any fatigue throughout eternity? No. All fatigue arises from the use of bodily organs by the thinking subject; spiritual activities in themselves are not subject to any fatigue; hence, the act of loving will not engender any weariness in the blessed throughout eternity.

Since our ultimate happiness consists in this perfect satisfaction of the faculties of our spiritual life, we can well understand why the term most commonly used in the Scriptures for Heaven is *life*. It occurs in this sense about one hundred times in the New Testament, in the majority of cases followed by the adjective *everlasting*. It is remarkable that it occurs in this sense in every book and letter of the New Testament, even in the short letter of St. Jude, with the sole exception of the letter to Philemon. It must have been the standing expression on the lips of Christ and His Apostles. In St. Matthew, St. Mark, and St. Luke, the term *kingdom of God* is more usually employed, whereas St. John almost exclusively uses *life* and speaks only twice of the kingdom. St. Paul uses *life* more frequently than *kingdom*.

What is the origin and the bearing of this term *life* for heavenly bliss, and why is it so often characterized as "everlasting"?

The origin lies beyond doubt in the Old Testament. In the Garden of Eden was planted the tree of life. The penalty for sin was death, and after the Fall, God sent Adam out of Paradise, "lest perhaps he put forth his hand, and take also of the tree of life, and eat, and live forever."[18]

The New Testament closes with a distinct reference to the opening of the Old: "Blessed are they that wash their robes in the blood of the Lamb: that they may have a right

[18] Gen. 3:22.

to the tree of life."[19] In the Psalms, the way of the just is called the *way of life*. In our Lord's day, the current expression for man's celestial reward was already *everlasting life*. This current expression was used by Christ and the Apostles, and endowed with greater fullness of meaning.

St. John especially, and also St. Paul, elaborate this theme of life everlasting. The Fourth Gospel says of the Word: "In Him was life, and the life was the light of men. And the light shineth in the darkness, and the darkness did not comprehend it."[20]

This life which is in God the Word will be bestowed on men:

He who heareth my word and believeth Him that sent me hath life everlasting, and cometh not into judgment, but is passed from death to life. Amen, amen, I say unto you, that the hour cometh, and now is, when the dead shall hear the voice of the Son of God; and they that hear shall live. For, as the Father hath life in Himself, so He hath given to the Son also to have life in Himself.[21]

[19] Apoc. 22:14 (RSV = Rev. 22:14).
[20] John 1:4-5.
[21] John 5:24-26.

As the living Father hath sent me and I live by the Father, so he that eateth me, the same also shall live by me. This is the bread that came down from Heaven.[22]

According to the Gospel of St. John, this life has indeed already begun in the hearts of the faithful on earth, although it comes to completion only when Christ raises those who believe in Him, on the last day. It consists in sharing the very life that the Father has in Himself and gives to the Son, who bestows it on those who are united to Him.

This life is light, mental light. "This is everlasting life that they should *know* Thee, the only true God, and Jesus Christ, whom Thou hast sent."[23] The knowledge of the Father and the Son is the light of men, their ultimate end and everlasting life.

It is called everlasting life, clearly, not merely on the ground that it will never come to an end, but that from its very nature it cannot come to an end. It is the fullness of life without the germ of death.

[22] John 6:58-59 (RSV = John 6:57-58).
[23] John 17:3.

The Greek adjective *aionios*, which is translated "everlasting," implies more than that it never ends; it suggests another kind of life than that which we naturally live on earth. It is the life of the *aion* — ("the age") to come; it is eternal life or the life in eternity, as Christ promised: "There is no man who hath left house or brethren or sisters or father or mother or children or lands, for my sake and for the gospel, who shall not receive a hundred times as much, now in this time . . . and in the world [*aion*] to come, life everlasting [*aionios*]."[24]

It is distinctly stated that the life hereafter will be not only endless, but timeless. "The angel lifted up his hand to Heaven and swore by Him that liveth forever and ever that time shall be longer."[25]

The reward, therefore, foretold in the New Testament is a timeless and changeless life akin to that of God, who "dwelleth in eternity [*aiona*]"[26] and who said, "Yea, I lift up my hand to Heaven and say: I am living forever [unto the *aion*]."[27]

[24] Cf. Mark 10:29-30.
[25] Apoc. 10:5-6 (RSV = Rev. 10:5-6).
[26] Cf. Isa. 57:15.
[27] Cf. Deut. 32:40.

This timeless divine life is in Christ, and Christ communicates it to others through the truth, which, when possessed, issues into life. Hence, Christ said of Himself, "I am the way, the truth, and the life. I am the light of the world. He that followeth me walketh not in darkness, but shall have the light of life."[28]

[28] John 14:6; 8:12.

❦

Chapter Three

What will I enjoy in Heaven?

In Heaven, we shall see Christ, not merely His Godhead, but also in His manhood. Christ in His human nature will constitute after the Beatific Vision, or, rather, *in* the Beatific Vision, the chief delight of the blessed. The three years' companionship of the Apostles with Christ on earth will be as nothing compared with the companionship of the blessed with Christ in Heaven.

In meditating on Heaven, one is apt to think of Christ as a great King in His glory sitting at the right hand of God the Father, a king to be worshiped with all due honor. No doubt in a sense this is true. The angels and the blessed hold court around His throne. In a way beyond our conception, the host of Heaven will pay obeisance and homage to Christ as King. Some analogy to what on earth we call ceremonial is suggested by the description of Heaven in St. John's book of Revelation. But these state occasions, if such one may dare to call them, do not exhaust celestial delights. Although Christ is the great King, He will also be the intimate personal friend of each of the blessed.

How this will be achieved we cannot say. On earth in Holy Communion, each recipient receives Christ whole and entire, even though thousands receive Him at the same time. If this multiplication of Christ's Real Presence is a fact during the state of our probation here below, we may infer that in Heaven Christ will find some means, now unknown to us, to be in close intimacy and individual companionship with each person in that multitude that no one can number. In Holy Communion, we only perceive His presence through the act of faith; hereafter, when faith has ceased, the real presence of His manhood in immediate proximity to each one of the saints must be immediately perceptible, and after the general resurrection, no doubt in some way sensible to human eyes. We have Christ's promise: "If any man shall hear my voice and open to me the door, I will come in to him and will sup with him and he with me."[29] If this is true during our mortal life, it must be truer still in our glorified state.

[29] Apoc. 3:20 (RSV = Rev. 3:20).

Christ Himself compared the kingdom of Heaven to a wedding feast prepared by a king for his son, and on several occasions Christ refers to Himself as the bridegroom. It is plain from the Scriptures that Christ's bride is the Church, which He loves and for which He delivered Himself to death. This is true of the Church whether Suffering, Militant, or Triumphant, but especially so of the Church Triumphant. St. John heard one of the seven angels say to him, "Come, and I will show thee the bride, the wife of the Lamb,"[30] whereupon the angel showed him the holy city, Jerusalem, coming down out of Heaven from God. The Lamb signifies beyond doubt Christ in His humanity, for only in His humanity was He slain and became the victim for our sins. Heaven is therefore described as the eternal nuptials of Christ in His humanity with the community of the redeemed.

This close union, however, is fully achieved only by the union of Christ to the individual blessed. On earth, the Church has always designated the individual soul as the spouse of Christ, for the kingdom of God is within us. The banquet of this wedding feast is, here below, the reception of the Body and Blood of Christ in the Blessed Sacrament.

[30] Apoc. 21:9-10 (RSV = Rev. 21:9-10).

This is a pledge of future glory when Christ in His humanity will be united with each of the saints in an everlasting intimacy and mutual friendship. We may, perhaps, have envied Mary the thirty years of hidden life that she spent with Jesus in the holy house of Nazareth, but in a sense this privilege will be surpassed when we are risen with Christ and possess the things that are above, where Christ is sitting at the right hand of God; when we mind the things that are above and no longer the things that are on earth; when we have died to this mortal life and our life is hidden with Christ in God, although we appear with Him in glory. This hiddenness does not involve any secrecy toward our fellow saints, but it means a uniqueness, a separateness of our own communion with Christ, a communion that is in no way troubled by the intrusion of others.

The humanity of Christ is hypostatically united to the Person of God the Son, and the Beatific Vision, which shows us God the Son, shows us the glory and lovableness of the manhood He assumed. The communion with the sacred humanity of Christ is the first and foremost thing mediated through the Beatific Vision. After the general resurrection, even our bodily eyes will rejoice in the sight of God incarnate, and our ears delight in His voice.

By what divine ingenuity this sacred humanity will be rendered quasi-omnipresent in Heaven we cannot at present say. We know only that the saints will "stand before the throne [the unveiled Godhead] and before the Lamb [God incarnate],"[31] that their songs will perpetually rise "to God and to the Lamb," and that the Lamb, standing before the throne, "'will shepherd" the saints. We know that the heavenly city has no temple — that is, no limited or in any way defined or circumscribed presence of God where He wishes to be worshiped. "For the Lord God Almighty is the temple thereof and the Lamb. And the city hath no need of the sun, nor of the moon, to shine in it. For the glory of God hath enlightened it and the Lamb is the lamp thereof."[32]

꙳

*Will I see anyone
other than God in Heaven?*

After the sight of God in His divine and in His human nature comes the joy of eternal companionship with the citizens of Heaven. To enter into Heaven is to enter into a

[31] Cf. Apoc. 7:9 (RSV = Rev. 7:9).
[32] Apoc. 21:22-23 (RSV = Rev. 21:22-23).

real community life, into social interchange and permanent association with Mary, the Mother of Jesus, and with the angels and the saints. Conceivably God might have made the eternal happiness of all spirits a merely personal, self-contained, and isolated state of bliss; He might have left celestial joy and eternal life a merely individual joy and individual life. But He has not done so.

It is the deep conviction of all Catholics that, on Calvary, Mary, the Mother of God, was made the mother of all the faithful whom her Son redeemed. This spiritual motherhood is exercised not merely by her perpetual intercession for us, while we are working out our salvation in fear and trembling, but continues in Heaven, where our love for her and her love for us is the cause of our principal joy, after that of loving her Son.

The whole angel world also will enhance our happiness. It is commonly accepted that the blessed will occupy the thrones left vacant by the fall of Lucifer and his followers; this means that we shall enter into fraternal communion with cherubim and seraphim and all the members of the heavenly host. Our contemplation of these mighty firstborn sons of God, the splendor of their intelligence, and the greatness of their love for Him and for us will fill us with joy.

According to Catholic teaching, each of the faithful on earth has his guardian angel. This angel, by perpetual guidance and intercession, is a ministering spirit to the soul entrusted to him for everlasting salvation. The bond of affection and intimacy between this celestial guardian and his ward will surely be transformed into a bond of special love and gratitude during eternity.

We know that God has arranged the angel host in "choirs." This means the angels are related to one another in some definite ordered way, having different and distinct rank and status, dignity, and special powers. They combine together into one great harmony of divine praise. They are not mere units; they are fellows in a divine college.

So it is likewise with the blessed redeemed. They form "a church," the Church Triumphant. They are not a crowd, but a heavenly army. Each redeemed soul has its post and position assigned. Heaven is a commonwealth where divine order reigns. "The Jerusalem which is above"[33] is a city-state, and its inhabitants are citizens. "'Our citizenship is in Heaven,"[34] wrote St. Paul.

[33] Gal. 4:26.
[34] Cf. Phil. 3:20.

Among the blessed themselves there will be the fellowship begotten of mutual respect, admiration, and intimate communion.

Moreover, human nature in Heaven is still human nature, however glorified. There will be ties of friendship between the saints. St. Augustine has met St. Ambrose and rejoiced. St. Francis has met St. Clare and found delight in communion with her. We also shall find among the saints in Heaven our friends whom we loved and venerated on earth. Christ on earth formed friendships, although He possessed the Beatific Vision. He loved John, and Mary and Martha and Lazarus. So, too, among the blessed, friendships will persist.

And again: after the resurrection the blessed will possess their bodies. This implies that they will have eyes to see, ears to hear, lips to speak, and so on. There must therefore be in Heaven something to see, to hear, and some persons to speak to, and these faculties are best and most fully exercised in a community that will enjoy heavenly bliss in fellowship. The unbroken comradeship with those of our own nature and race is part of the complete development of our manhood. In the center of this fellowship is Christ in His human nature, for the Incarnation remains forever the link by which men are bound together.

In Christ we are all brethren, not merely on earth, but throughout eternity.

❧

Will I see the beauties of Creation?

Besides the sight and love of God and Christ, and the company of Mary, angels, and saints, the blessed will enjoy all the wonders of creation. Until the last day, they will know this present world; after the last day, when this Heaven and this earth shall have passed away, they will know the new heavens and the new earth that will be the everlasting abode of the saints of God.

In the book of Revelation of St. John we find set forth in exuberant imagery the glories of the New Jerusalem, the city of God. Perhaps the streets of gold and the crystal sea before the throne of God, the gates and the walls of precious stones, the crowns and the palms, and the costly robes are metaphors, and not to be taken literally. But, if so, they must be metaphors for a reality that far exceeds our greatest expectations. St. Paul says that "all creation groaneth and travaileth in pain . . . waiting for the adoption of the sons of God."[35] The material creation that will

[35] Rom. 8:22-23.

be the eternal home of the blessed will be a universe at least not less marvelous than the vast universe in which we now live. God has in Christ united with Himself a material body, in which forever Christ will sit at the right hand of His Father. God has decreed the resurrection of man's body, and thereby determined the eternal existence of a material universe in which the Redeemer and the Redeemed will live and move for all eternity.

If it may be said of this present world, "The Heavens show forth the glory of God, and the firmament declareth the work of His hands. Day unto day uttereth speech and night unto night showeth knowledge,"[36] this must be true in an unspeakably higher degree of the world to come. Questions have been asked about this new earth, whether it will have a silvery sea and a starry sky; whether it will contain rivers and mountains, animals and plants. To all these questions we have no answer, for God has not deigned to reveal it to us. But one thing we know: it will be a real world and a fit abode for men and women to whom are restored the days of Paradise when God walked with man in the Garden of Eden in the cool of the evening. Although the essential happiness of Heaven lies in

[36] Ps. 18:2-3 (RSV = Ps. 19:1-2).

the sight and enjoyment of God, we may also say of such lesser joys as the enjoyment of the marvels of creation that "no eye hath ever seen, nor ear heard, neither hath it entered into the heart of man, what things God has prepared for those that love Him."[37]

We must remember, however, that our enjoyment of the glories of nature will differ in Heaven from our enjoyment of natural beauties now. Now we find it difficult to see the Creator in the things He has created. Our reason tells us that all creation is but a manifestation of God, but owing to the limitation of our minds and our natural inability directly to see God, our very attention to the grandeurs of nature may obscure our realization of God.

It will be different in Heaven. All things will be seen and admired in the Beatific Vision as in a mirror. The thought of God will never be absent from our minds even for a second, although our mind and body may be occupied with the beauty of the things He made. The whole of creation will be as a constant song praising Him, who called it out of nothing into being. Every created thing will be as the fragment of crystal in which a ray of the infinite light is reflected.

[37] 1 Cor. 2:9.

What kind of body will I have in Heaven?

The glory of man's body in Heaven will be the natural consequence of the glory of the soul. The body was intended to be the handmaid of the soul, ministering in every way to its spiritual life. This relation between body and soul was disturbed through the Fall. The dominion of spirit over matter was rudely shaken, and the flesh became the unwilling partner of the mind. Its sluggishness and its passions were a continual hindrance to the full development of the soul's life. This will completely cease in Heaven.

Man's body will then be a furtherance to his spiritual joys. The joys of the soul will overflow and fill the material side of his being with the most exquisite happiness. Great mental happiness sometimes even on earth buoys up man's physical frame and gives it a feeling of vigor and lightsomeness, and is the cause of, maintenance of, or restoration to bodily health, even as sorrow is the cause of disease and death. The supreme bliss of Heaven proceeding from the soul will pervade the body to such an extent that its physical well being will exceed anything we have known on earth.

Moreover, by special ordinance of God, the body will be so exalted that it will become a worthy companion to the soul in possession of the sight of God. As Christ was transfigured on Mount Thabor, so that His face shone as the sun and His garments were white as snow, so shall all those who are co-heirs with Christ be glorified in body as well as in soul. The body will receive those preternatural gifts, of which the gifts to Adam in Paradise were but a foretaste.

Chapter Five

✺

What is Heaven like?

Heaven is frequently described in the Scriptures as a kingdom:

> I dispose to you, as my Father hath disposed to me, a kingdom; that you may eat and drink at my table, in my kingdom.[38]

> Come, ye blessed of my Father, and possess the kingdom prepared for you from the foundation of the world.[39]

> At the end of the world . . . the Son of man shall send His angels, and they shall gather out of His

[38] Luke 22:29-30.
[39] Matt. 25:34.

kingdom all scandals and them that work iniquity, and shall cast them into a furnace of fire; there shall be weeping and gnashing of teeth. Then shall the just shine as the sun in the kingdom of their Father.[40]

The Lord God shall enlighten them, and they shall reign forever and ever.[41]

To him that shall overcome, I will give to sit with me in my throne, as I also have overcome and am set down with my Father in His throne.[42]

In Christ all shall be made alive, but every one in his own order: the firstfruits, Christ; then they that are of Christ, who have believed in His coming. Afterward the end, when He shall have delivered up the kingdom to God and the Father: when He shall have brought to nought all principality and power and virtue. For He must reign until He hath put all His enemies under His feet. . . . When all things shall be subdued unto Him, then the Son

[40] Matt. 11:40-43.

[41] Apoc. 22:5 (RSV = Rev. 22:5).

[42] Apoc. 3:21 (RSV = Rev. 3:21).

also Himself shall be subject unto Him [the Father] that put all things under Him, that God may be all in all."[43]

Hence also St. John in his vision of Heaven saw thrones set, and the ancients with crowns on their heads, and he said, "The prince of the Kings of the earth . . . hath made us a kingdom and priests to God and His Father, to Him be glory and empire forever and ever."[44]

This kingship promised to the blessed in the Scriptures involves first of all a manifest triumph and undoubted victory over all adverse powers, over the devils and the damned that tempted them and endeavored to hinder them in the attainment of their final end, over the obstacles that stood in their way through the frailty of their own nature and the greatness of their task.

The blessed will be like Alpine travelers, who have at last reached the dazzling heights. They have attained the very summit of their desires, notwithstanding the storms that raged, the foes that waylaid them, and the steepness of the path they climbed.

[43] 1 Cor. 15:22-25, 28.
[44] Apoc. 1:5-6 (RSV = Rev. 1:5-6).

It includes, further, an untrammeled freedom during eternity, a full liberty and immediate fulfillment of their wishes, and a complete disposal of all the riches of their royal inheritance without any possibility of being thwarted or gainsaid.

It includes, lastly, a real dominion over all creation. At the final consummation, after the resurrection of the body, they will have a complete mastery over all material things, and all nature will obey them and submit to their sovereignty. Even in the spiritual world of angels and fellow saints they will reign, for they will be as princes among princes, all of whom in celestial courtesy will pay honor to one another. With utter spontaneity and eagerness, all will serve God, to serve whom is to reign.

When St. Paul says that, at the end, Christ will deliver up the kingdom to the Father and be subject to Him, he means that Christ in His manhood, as head of the human race, with all His brethren, with all those redeemed by His Blood, with all those who were saved in Him and through Him, will proclaim the full achievement of the Father's will.

Before His Passion, Christ declared, "Father, I have finished the work which Thou gavest me to do; and now glorify Thou me, Father, with the glory which I had with

Thee before the world was made. . . . I pray for them . . . whom thou hast given me out of the world. . . . I pray for those who, through their word, shall believe in me, that they all should be one, as I in Thee and Thou in me."[45]

At the final consummation, Christ will proclaim in regard to His celestial life what He said at the end of His mortal life: "I have finished the work which Thou gavest me to do, and now glorify Thou me." This handing over of the kingdom means the public acknowledgment of the completed work of Christ. The first petition of the Lord's Prayer — "Hallowed be Thy name; Thy kingdom come" — will have been fully granted.

After the final consummation, one phase of Christ's activity will cease. Christ's life in Heaven is now one of perpetual intercession for us.[46] Then no more intercession will be needed. Christ's daily sacrifice of the altar is one of propitiation and impetration for the living and the dead; in Heaven, it will be offered for those purposes no longer. The sacraments are the channels of Christ's Precious Blood to the souls of men; they will require these channels no longer. Christ is on earth the Teacher of men through

[45] Cf. John 17:4-5, 9, 20-21.
[46] Rom. 8:34; Heb. 7:25.

the infallible authority of the Church; they will need that authority no longer. Christ is the Captain of salvation in the great warfare of the Militant Church, but the soldiers will then need their general no longer, for the war will have been won. In one sense, therefore, the final consummation is an abdication of Christ, and a handing back of the emblems of office to His heavenly Father.

On the other hand, Christ continues to reign in a higher sense. Christ continues eternally to be the head of the human race, and in their life of glory, He is their leader. All the blessed are what they are through Him. On earth, to be in grace means to be in Christ; in Heaven, to be in glory means to be in Christ in an even more complete sense.

The Church Triumphant is still Christ's Mystical Body. The blessed are in glory through their unbroken union with Him. What Christ said on earth remains true in Heaven: "I am the vine; you are the branches."[47] The Beatific Vision is given to the saints because of Christ and in Christ. They need a mediator of propitiation or intercession no longer, for they are eternally sinless and have no wants for which such prayer need be offered. But if they

[47] John 15:5.

are heirs of God, they are also co-heirs of Christ, and their inheritance is not bestowed upon them independently of Christ. They are heirs of God — that is, they possess the light of glory because their human nature is the same as that of Christ and supernaturally united with it.

The Hypostatic Union of God the Son with the human nature of Christ is the foundation of all honor and blessings that come upon men, who are brethren according to the flesh of God incarnate. Christ, on the eve of His Passion, said to His Father: "I also have given unto them the glory which Thou hast given unto me, that they may be one, as we also are one: I in them and Thou in me; that they may be perfect in one."[48] The glory the Father gives to Christ is the glory of divine Sonship. The Father gives this glory to the Son in the blessed Trinity by the communication of His divine nature, for the Son is the splendor of the Father. The Father gives this glory to the humanity of Christ by the Hypostatic Union of Christ's human nature to the Son of God. And, again, the Father gives it to the human mind of Christ by the Beatific Vision.

Neither the divine Sonship in the Trinity nor the Hypostatic Union is communicable to us creatures, but

[48] John 17:22-23.

the Beatific Vision is. This is the glory Christ obtained for us from the Father. It is given to us both by the Father and the Son; hence, the words of Christ: "I also have given"; for in giving them sanctifying grace, Christ had already given them the seed of glory. Christ could say this not merely as God but also as God incarnate, for His human nature is the link that binds us to Him and Him to us; hence, He could say, "I in them and Thou in me," that thus through Christ we may be perfected into one and God may be all in all.

⚜

Is Heaven an actual place?

Is Heaven a real place? Yes. Christ ascended into Heaven, and from thence He shall come to judge. Numerous texts of Scripture, which it would be tedious to quote, make it plain that Heaven is a locality into which one enters and from which one can depart. St. John's description of Heaven as a city with walls is no doubt imaginary and metaphorical, but it would be altogether deceptive unless Heaven were a place in some way circumscribed and limited. Moreover, Christ, who has a real material body, is in Heaven. This body, however glorified and capable of moving with the speed of light, is a real extended measurable, visible body, and therefore in some physical relation to space.

Now, Christ has prayed, "Father, I pray that where I shall be, they may also be." He said to Peter, "You cannot follow me now, but you shall follow hereafter."[49] It is therefore, and always has been, the universal conviction of Catholics that Heaven is a definite place in the universe. In this place are now at least two material bodies, those of Jesus and Mary, His Mother, and there will the saved be in their glorified bodies after the general resurrection.

A difficulty naturally arises with regard to the presence of the disembodied souls of the saved previous to the resurrection. Of those souls, this may be said: they cannot be localized by material extension, as if they could be measured and had length, breadth, or depth, or could be divided into parts. For these souls, although they are the animating principle of material bodies, are themselves spiritual. They are therefore in a place in a similar way to that in which angels are in a place: they are present in virtue of their activity. The blessed, therefore, even before the resurrection, are with Christ, who is in Heaven. This has to be understood in a local and spatial sense.

[49] John 13:36.

How precisely that presence is effected and what it implies escape our experience and knowledge.

⚜

Will friendships and family
ties remain in Heaven?

In Heaven, the blessed will see all things in God and God in all things. They will see all things in that divine order in which they stand in God's mind. Their place and position in the universe that God created will be understood, for the outlook of the saints on all things will resemble that of God.

The same principle governs the love of the blessed for all the creatures of God's hand. They love them in God, and for God's sake. Their love for them is only a particular mode and application of their love for God.

Now, in this divine law of charity, they observe due order. On earth, there is a double principle that rules the due measure of charity toward one's neighbor. First, the neighbor's own goodness — that is, his own share in the goodness of God or his proximity to God. Secondly, his proximity to ourselves; thus, we must love parents, children, our kith and kin, and our countrymen more than strangers. Such is the law of nature and the law of God.

In that beatific charity, which is the counterpart of the Beatific Vision, there can be but one principle that rules the measure of love, and that is the share in divine goodness that each saint possesses in his own particular degree. But this beatific charity is supernatural, and the supernatural does not destroy the natural, but perfects it. Hence, the blessed will feel greater natural affection toward some persons than toward others. A son will be moved with love toward his mother; a mother will thrill with joy at the sight of her child. Nature in Heaven is hallowed and made perfect in charity, which as a simple proverb says, "begins at home."

Our Lord on earth ever possessed the Beatific Vision in a higher degree than any of the saints; yet He had a disciple "whom He loved";[50] he had a home at Bethany where Mary, Martha, and Lazarus lived, who were above others beloved. Our Lord, now in Heaven, loves His Mother supremely in the Beatific Vision for her holiness, since, indeed, she is the holiest of all creatures. But in addition to this, He also loves her with a perfect natural love because she is His Mother, and in the natural order also His love for her is supreme. Our Lord will be the example for all the

[50] John 13:23; 19:26.

saints; they also will love their parents and their brethren, as He loves His.

The blessed, then, will still love creatures, but their love will be as pure and as sinless as Christ's own. The saints are of necessity impeccable. They can sin no more. To sin would be to prefer some created good above God, and this is utterly impossible to them.

They actually see and possess the Sovereign Good itself. Their will clings to Him as a magnet to iron. Once in Heaven, they leave all sin and all consequence of sin behind; their wills are confirmed in glory; every act, word, and deed must be holy, and holy with absolute ease and spontaneity.

The saints, then, will love their fellow saints with an intensity and tenderness beyond any love we can experience on earth, and they will love them each in his proper degree and be loved by them in return to the utmost extent conformable to their sanctity and kinship.

※

Will Heaven be the
same for each person?

No, Heaven will not be the same for all. As in the firmament, star differs from star in glory, so also is it in the heavenly abode of the blessed. The principle of celestial happiness will always be the same — namely, the sight of God face-to-face — and the happiness even of the lowliest saint will immeasurably exceed what we can now imagine. Yet their glory and happiness will differ.

The gift of the Beatific Vision will be bestowed on the blessed in unequal measure, according to their merits. It is sometimes asked whether those who upon earth were gifted with great intelligence or who possessed great erudition, and therefore great stores of knowledge, will in Heaven have some advantage above those who on earth were dull and ignorant. The answer is not far to seek. Neither natural genius nor acquired knowledge will in itself have any influence upon the degree of glory bestowed by God as a supernatural gift.

Our blessed Lady, as far as her mere natural powers go, is far inferior to the angels of God — the angelic nature is higher than the human — yet no one, not even the highest of the Seraphim, has such a deep knowledge of God as His blessed Mother, for her knowledge is the fruit of the grace received. St. Thomas well remarks, "He shares more fully in the light of glory who possesses the greater love; for where love is greater, there is greater desire, and desire in some way renders him who desires apt and ready to receive the object desired. Hence, he who has more love will see God more perfectly and be more blessed."[51] This inequality of heavenly glory has been solemnly defined by the Council of Trent[52] against the Reformers, who sought the root of justification in the imputed merits of Christ and, as these are equal for all, could not admit varying degrees of reward in Heaven.

Moreover, the knowledge of creatures obtained here on earth even by the greatest mind, is of an inferior kind to that obtained by the humblest saint in the Beatific Vision. In the Beatific Vision, they are seen in a higher and more perfect way: they are seen in the cause that produces them, in God who conceived them and gives them existence. In comparison with this intuitive knowledge, earthly sense knowledge and discursive reasoning will be as candlelight in the presence of the noonday sun.

If the glory of the saints is unequal, will not regret enter the hearts of those saints who have received less because they merited less? Will they feel no pang and bitterness of soul in having, through their own fault, lost a higher

[51] St. Thomas Aquinas (c. 1225-1274; Dominican philosopher, theologian, and Doctor), *Summa Theologica*, I, Q. 12, art. 6.

[52] Session 9, can. 32.

degree of eternal happiness? No, for each will receive to the utmost of his own capacity. They will all drink from the fountain of life, although some will have but a tiny cup and others an ampler vessel. Regret and sorrow is possible only where there is frustration of desire. There can be no such disappointment in Heaven, for God will make every soul happy to the utmost of its power, even though the power of one soul for happiness will be greater than that of another. Even the humblest saint will so love God that he will rejoice that God is known and loved by another saint with greater love than his own.

꙼

Do the blessed feel for those on earth?

First of all, do the blessed know what happens on earth?

We must distinguish the state of the blessed before and after the general resurrection. Before the resurrection, these souls are without their bodies, and therefore without the natural means of communication with the outer world. Whether a soul purely in the natural order would, by its own power, be able to know something outside itself during its separation from the body, we cannot say with any certainty. We are dealing, however, not with the natural order, but with the supernatural; we are dealing with souls that have received the Beatific Vision.

What knowledge does God, as a matter of fact, grant them according to His good pleasure? We have to guide us, first of all, the fact that the Church authorizes and encourages prayers to the saints — not only saints canonized by the Church, but to any persons of whom we have reasonable hope that they are in Heaven. This directly involves the truth that those in Heaven know when they are addressed by those on earth; it also implies that they have sufficient cognizance of all the circumstances which alone can make those prayers intelligible to them. When a person on earth utters a cry for help to any saint, it is obviously not required that he should first mentally or verbally explain what particular distress is the cause of his cry.

We have further to guide us the fact that the angels know in detail what happens on earth. "There is more joy before the angels of God upon one sinner that does penance than upon ninety-nine who need not penance."[53] Christ threatened those who gave scandal to the little ones, "for their angels ever see the face of my Father who

[53] Luke 15:7.

is in Heaven."[54] The angel world, therefore, has cognizance of earthly affairs, as they are "ministering angels sent to help those who have received the inheritance of salvation." As the blessed share the Beatific Vision with the angels and are their companions, it is unnatural to suppose that they should be in ignorance of what their companions in Heaven know.

It is an axiom in theology that grace does not destroy nature. It is true still more that glory does not destroy but exalts and sanctifies nature. It would be unnatural if the departed had no wish to know at least some matters connected with those they loved and still love on earth. It cannot be supposed that God, who grants them the Beatific Vision, would hide from them what they must naturally desire to know.

The saints, therefore, know, and the saints care for the welfare of those on earth. They care for their temporal welfare, their health and their sickness, their poverty and their well-being, their honor and their dishonor. But they care for these things only as a means to an end. That end is the eternal salvation and the higher glory of those whom they love.

[54] Matt. 18:10.

The saints see all things from the standpoint of eternity. If bitter sufferings, even in those who are nearest and dearest to them, are God's instruments for the purification and sanctification of their souls, the saints will not ask for their removal, lest the everlasting happiness of their future companions be lessened. The saints love their own, but with a spiritual, supernatural love, that does not shrink from seeing suffering, if suffering is the path to glory.

The saints, then, desire the good of the souls of those who are their kith and kin on earth. What if they see them in spiritual danger — if they see them sin? They continue their intercession for them at the throne of God.

But is there anxiety and sorrow in Heaven on account of temptation and of sin on earth? No, there cannot be. God has wiped all tears from their eyes; they can feel sorrow no longer. They have so completely surrendered to God's blessed will, their resignation is so complete, their loving jubilant adoration of God's will so perfect, that nothing can disturb their souls' happy calm.

Perhaps a reader might think, "But Christ suffered; Christ had His agony in the Garden, although His resignation was utterly perfect. Why, then, cannot saints suffer still at the sight of sin on earth?" The answer lies in the mystery of the Incarnation. Although Christ's soul ever saw the face of His Father in Heaven, yet His body was still mortal and passible on earth. Christ, then, as regards the fullness of His manhood — I mean body and soul together — was still a wayfarer on earth, even though His soul saw God in the Beatific Vision. The saints are no longer wayfarers; they have reached the land of the living, where sorrow cannot enter.

Let us remember, however, that although the saints cannot suffer, they can, until the final consummation after the Last Day, still increase in what theologians call their *accidental happiness.* They can truly long and intensely wish for the salvation of those who are near and dear to them — in fact, for the salvation of all men. Hence, they can pray, they can plead with God, and the doctrine of the Communion of Saints makes us certain that they do.

When men sin on earth, do the saints feel angry with them and call down punishment on the offender? They indeed hate sin, but they do not hate the sinner, for the sinner on earth, however vile, is never beyond God's mercy, and until the moment when God Himself has uttered the verdict of eternal damnation against the sinner, the saints cannot but continue their prayers for those for whom the Blood of Christ still speaks better than that of Abel.

Do the blessed feel for those in Hell?

It is often asked how the saints can be happy when they know that some, even perchance those who were near and dear to them, are in Hell. Will a mother lose the love for her son and be indifferent to his loss? The difficulty is one not so much of logic and reason, but of sentiment.

The love of mother for child has its first beginnings in mere animal nature. Even the beast of the field "loves" its young. This instinctive tendency in man is lifted to the rational plane. A human mother loves her son because, although his soul was directly created by God, his human nature, a compound of body and soul, is derived from her. She collaborated in the building up of that manhood, and his very substance is derived from her. He is her own image and likeness, committed for many years to her care, and thus in another way also her own handiwork. This natural rational love can remain, as we have seen, even in eternity.

But as the blessed are sinless, all their rational acts are in perfect conformity with God's will. The love of God is the one dominating power in their eternal life. The very greatness of that love casts out every sentiment incompatible with it. Nothing can become the object of love except in as far as it is good and lovable.

Now, the damned have nothing good or lovable in them, since they deliberately and everlastingly reject God, the Sovereign Good. Hence, they have ceased to be possible objects of anyone's love. They are utterly unlovable.

Perhaps it will be pleaded that at least mothers do not cease to love ugly and unlovable children, however repugnant to strangers. But in this objection lurks an ambiguity. True, a mother loves a child in spite of his external ugliness, because, looking below the surface, she sees some lovable characteristics that escape the notice of others. When, however, we deal with moral depravity, the case is somewhat different. The knowledge of inner moral depravity normally lessens even a mother's love. Agrippina's love for her son Nero, when she succumbed to his second attempt of assassination, had obviously lessened.

However, it is true that on earth even the moral depravity of the son does but rarely extinguish a mother's love completely. The reason for this is twofold. The depravity is never total. A mother's ingenuity will discover a redeeming trait even in a monster of iniquity. Furthermore, the depravity is not beyond the possibility of change. The mother hopes that her son's better self will one day triumph, be that hope ever so faint, that day ever so distant. Make the depravity total, make it everlasting, and even a mother's love dies, for there remains nothing more to love. The damned are outside the bond of charity.

Opponents of Christianity often consider it horrible that the saints are said to rejoice in the punishment of the damned. But here, again, we are dealing with an ambiguity. The saints do not rejoice in the pains of the damned as such. The agony of the lost, viewed in itself, cannot be the cause of pleasure to any right-minded creature, least of all to the saints in Heaven.

But they rejoice in the fact that justice is being done, that God should withdraw Himself from those who hate Him, and thus cause the pain of loss, that those who prefer the creature to the creator should find in the creature their torment and undergo the pain of sense. They see in this the manifestation of infinite holiness, and they rejoice that it is so. God wills it, and they will it with Him, for all that God wills is right and everlastingly to be praised.

Moreover, they, the blessed, know that they themselves were once on trial and in danger of being lost. Having triumphed, and being in everlasting light, they are not afraid to gaze into that darkness from which they are saved.

Lastly, the damned are not merely the foes of God. In hating God, they hate all the good, because they are good and united to God. Hence, the good in union with God are united with Him in eternal opposition to the wicked.

Chapter Six

※

Will I have to wait for heavenly rewards?

In earliest times, there were some who, misled by certain texts in the book of Revelation and by the strange fancies of Jewish-Christian circles, exemplified in Papias early in the second century, imagined that after the general resurrection, a reign of Christ with the risen saints would be established here on earth for a thousand years. Only after the expiration of this period would the saints enter Heaven in consummated bliss. At the first resurrection, only the just would rise and enter this earthly kingdom, in which they would be prepared by Christ for the final consummation, when they would contemplate the Father in His divine glory.

These ideas were held by some in East and West. Tertullian, Victorinus, and Lactantius among the Latin Fathers, and St. Irenaeus among the Greeks, were affected by them; but their very words betray that these fancies were not shared by all Christians. In fact, they were strongly opposed by many from the very beginning, and after some intermittent vogue during the first four centuries, were universally and definitely set aside within the Church. They would have been forever relegated to the curiosities of ancient literature, were it not for some revival of them among Protestant sects in recent years.

Quite apart, however, from this question of "the thousand years," or Millenarism, as it is called, there remains the uncertainty and ambiguity of some of the Fathers regarding the state of souls between death and the general judgment. It was indeed realized that neither their punishment nor their reward was full and complete until the Last Day, but wherein this incompleteness consisted was not clearly understood.

The point is not whether a definite judgment on the soul's eternal future immediately succeeds death — on this all were agreed — but whether this judgment is forthwith completely carried out. In reading the early Fathers, who speak of a delay after death, even for the saved, before they enter eternal bliss, we must remember that in many instances they are speaking of the holy souls in Purgatory, even though they may not use this technical term, but refer to them as the saints, the blessed, or the saved. Still, even after making allowance for such cases, there remain undoubted instances, especially of Greek Fathers, who postpone the bliss of Heaven for the saved until after the general judgment. They are not unanimous in their description of this state, whether it be a sleep, a rest, or some beginning of celestial happiness.

The bulk of Christian writers has always admitted some beginning of celestial happiness for the blessed immediately after death. The majority, again, of these admitted that this happiness consisted in the sight of God face-to-face; but even among these, there remained the question whether the Beatific Vision was of equal intensity before the resurrection of the body as it will be afterward.

This question is not peremptorily settled even today. St. Augustine, and after him St. Bernard, St. Bonaventure, and also St. Thomas in his earlier writings, held that before the general resurrection, the natural craving of the blessed for the possession of their bodies, and for the reconstitution of their complete human nature, involved some inhibition or retardation of the completeness of their union with God. Their soul, not being completely at rest within itself, is supposed to lack its utmost concentration upon God; the attention of the mind and the fervor of the will are supposed to be in some degree still capable of increase and lacking perfection.

St. Augustine, in his *Retractationes*, toward the end of his life felt not so certain about an affirmative answer to this question as he had felt in his younger years. So likewise St. Thomas seems to have changed his mind in later years. The Beatific Vision, he finally held, was always of equal intensity. The increase of happiness after the resumption of the risen body was one of greater extent, not intensity. The soul rejoiced that its glory extended also to the body.

The fact remains, acknowledged by all theologians, that the happiness of the blessed increases in some way after the general resurrection, although they possess the substance of their eternal bliss before.

Altogether apart from these questions debated among orthodox theologians, there was a minority of Christian writers, especially in the East, who did not even grant to the blessed the enjoyment of the Beatific Vision previous to the general judgment. Some few of these would use language that would suggest a state of sleep or unconscious rest for the saved until that day. They wrongly transferred the rest or sleep of the body in the grave to a supposed rest or sleep of the soul.

The greater number, on the other hand, would admit a real active life in these disembodied souls, but they invented a kind of intermediate state between earth and Heaven, consisting not in the Beatific Vision, but the enjoyment of the company of Christ. The dead were in Christ and with Christ, possessing a happiness far exceeding any happiness known on earth, yet not in possession of the Beatific Vision in Heaven.

Moreover, in the liturgy of St. John Chrysostom and in the Syriac liturgy, an ambiguity of expression occurs that would easily lead to the mistaken conviction that prayers were offered for the saints, and even for our blessed Lady, in company with the other faithful departed. This verbal ambiguity seems to have existed even in St. Augustine's time, who, in Sermon 159, says, "According to the discipline of the Church, as the faithful know, when the names of the martyrs are recited at the altar, no prayer is offered up for them, but prayer is offered for the other deceased whose names are mentioned. It would be an insult to pray for a martyr, by whose prayers we ourselves have to be commended to God."

Our prayer for the saints, therefore, asks not that they may obtain eternal happiness, but that their glory among men on earth may increase, that everywhere they may be recognized and honored as saints. For this accidental glory we may pray.

Perhaps also we pray for the glorification of their bodies, which they will possess in the general resurrection. This last prayer we may offer in the sense in which we say in the Lord's Prayer, "Thy kingdom come." The Father's kingdom has not come until all are glorified in Heaven in body as well as in soul.

Unsound views, however, about the state of the blessed previous to the judgment increased to a great extent in the Greek-speaking world. At the Council of Lyons, held in 1274 for the reunion of the Greeks with the Catholic Church, the opinion that Heaven is delayed until after the judgment had become predominant among those schismatic Christians. They were required to subscribe the following dogmatic formula: "The souls of those who, after receiving sacred Baptism, have incurred no stain whatever of sin, and also those who, after contracting the stain of sin, have been purified either while still remaining in their bodies, or divested of them, will be received forthwith into Heaven."[55]

[55] *The Profession of Faith Proposed to Michael Paleologus* (Denziger), 464.

Will I have to wait for heavenly rewards?

The question, however, was not completely settled by this decision, for it remained possible to discuss the precise meaning of the word *Heaven* in the decree. Forty years later, it was Pope John XXII who raised this question, and for a short time it was fiercely debated in Western Christendom. It was maintained by some that the souls of the saints were indeed with Christ in Heaven, and that their heavenly happiness had begun, but that until the Last Day they saw God only in the sacred humanity of Christ, and knew Him only as in a mirror, and by abstraction. The vision of God face-to-face was reserved for the final consummation after the general judgment.

For two or three years, the Pope himself seemed inclined to favor this view, although, even as a private teacher, apart from his supreme teaching office, he never held it or taught it definitely. He did, indeed, gather patristic opinions in favor of it; he often referred to it in public sermons, and for a time he regarded it as the more probable alternative.

As this roused the bitterest opposition in Europe, he seems gradually to have changed his mind, and on his deathbed, on December 3, 1334, he called the cardinals together and told them that he had drawn up a bull, of which this was the vital passage:

We confess and believe that the souls separated from the body and fully purified are in Heaven, in the kingdom of Heaven, in Paradise and with Jesus Christ in the company of the angels, and that according to the common law they see God and the divine Essence face-to-face and clearly, insofar as is in accordance with the state and condition of a separated soul.

His successor, Benedict XII, in an apostolic Constitution issued January 29, 1336, set the whole matter at rest by defining as follows:

They [disembodied souls] see the divine Essence with intuitive vision and face-to-face, no creature acting as a medium by way of object of vision; but the divine Essence shows itself to them directly, nakedly, clearly, and plainly, and thus seeing they enjoy this very divine Essence, and through such vision and fruition the souls of the dead are verily blessed and have life and rest eternal.

The reader will note that the qualifying final clause, which John XXII still thought it necessary to add in his dying declaration, is omitted. Benedict XII no longer says,

"Insofar as is in accordance with the state and condition of a separated soul." He states it absolutely and without qualification whatsoever. There is, in fact, no reason for any qualification, as the soul, even without the body, is completely capable of receiving the Beatific Vision.

In the light of this question, the following scriptural text requires some elucidation:

> I saw under the altar the souls of them that were slain for the word of God and for the testimony which they held. And they cried with a loud voice, saying, "How long, O Lord, holy and true, dost Thou not judge and revenge our blood on them that dwell on the earth?" And white robes were given, to every one of them. And it was said to them that they should rest for a little time till their fellow servants and their brethren, who are to be slain even as they, should be filled up.[56]

The martyrs here referred to, having died for Christ, are in Heaven and in enjoyment of the Beatific Vision, yet they are portrayed as praying that God may vindicate their blood. They are told to wait and to rest until the

---

[56] Apoc. 6:9-11 (RSV = Rev. 6:9-11).

number of martyrs is filled up. What does this mean? Are they in some distress, or is anything lacking to their happiness? Why are they under the altar? No altar indeed, is mentioned in the preceding text, yet the meaning is not far to seek.

Before the throne stands the Lamb, as it were, slain. This divine Victim is Christ, the Lamb who took away the sins of the world. The martyrs are slain because of Him. He is portrayed as standing, as though slain, because, having died a victim for sin, He is risen, and His glorified body, still carrying the wounds, stands on the altar before the throne.

The martyrs, like Him, are slain — and slain for His sake, but not as yet risen from the dead. Hence, they are portrayed as under His altar awaiting the resurrection of the body. Although dead in the body, they are living in soul; hence, a robe of glory is given to each one of them, the "light of glory" of the Beatific Vision. They are told to rest and wait until the final consummation of all things, when the last martyrs shall have died for Christ, and, entering into Heaven, complete the number of the saints. Then, at the general resurrection, their bodies, once slain for Christ, shall enter also into glory and their blood be fully vindicated.

It would be a mistake, therefore, to see in this text an indication of the delay of the Beatific Vision until after the day of the general judgment. The judgment here prayed for and the vindication of martyrs' blood is indeed the Last Judgment, and the manifest triumph of all the martyr-host on the Last Day. But it is not a request for their own personal and essential reward. This is symbolized by the white robes at once bestowed upon them and by the "rest" into which they enter. This rest is evidently the living, active rest of those who have entered everlasting life, that rest of which the letter to the Hebrews speaks,[57] when the blessed rest from their works as God did from His on the seventh day.

It is quite true that some Scripture texts imply that the bestowal of the final reward or punishment takes place at the Second Coming of Christ in the general judgment.[58] They do not, however, show that the Beatific Vision, and therefore the essence of heavenly bliss, is not granted to disembodied souls. It is indeed true that final blessedness and consummated glory are bestowed only when the soul rejoins the body. Only then, and not before, will our

[57] Heb. 4:7-10.
[58] See Matt. 25:31.

complete humanity receive its ultimate perfection and joy, and our blessed Lord's words will be fulfilled: "Come, ye blessed of my Father, possess ye the kingdom prepared for you from the foundation of the world."

On the other hand, it must be remembered that Christ on Good Friday was asked, "Lord, remember me when Thou shalt come into Thy kingdom," and answered, "Today thou shalt be with me in Paradise."[59] It is noteworthy that Christ did not use in His reply the phrase "in my kingdom," as the request of the penitent thief suggested. The fullness of Christ's kingship and the complete establishment of His kingdom takes place when, as man, He will rule over men in Heaven. His sway over disembodied souls is not the full manifestation of His royalty. Nevertheless, before that day, the blessed will be with Him in Paradise. The precise extent of this paradisial bliss with Christ the Scriptures do not define, although they suggest that it includes substantially and in essence man's great reward.

The immediacy of the celestial reward after death for those who are free from sin and its penalties clearly results also from these words of St. Paul:

[59] Cf. Luke 23:42-43.

If our earthly house of this habitation be dissolved, we have a building of God, a house not made with hands, eternal in Heaven. . . . We groan, desiring to be clothed upon with our habitation that is from Heaven, yet so that we be found clothed, not naked. . . . We, who are in this tabernacle groan, being burdened; because we would not be unclothed, but clothed upon, that that which is mortal may be swallowed up by life. . . . We have confidence, knowing that while we are in the body, we are absent from the Lord, for we walk by faith and not by sight; but we are confident and have a good will to be absent rather from the body and to be present with the Lord.[60]

The passage becomes clear when once the somewhat unusual phraseology is understood. Our earthly house is this mortal body; our heavenly house, our glorified body; the naked soul is the disembodied soul, possessing neither its earthly nor its celestial body. Here on earth, we groan at the thought of death because we would wish to exchange our mortal body straightway for our glorified one, and not

[60] 2 Cor. 5:1-8.

to pass through our naked state, divested of any body at all. Yet, although we dread death, we have "a good will to be absent rather from the body and to be present with the Lord." It is better for us to be with Christ, even though in a disembodied state, than to be in our bodies here away from Christ. To be away from Christ is to walk only by faith; to be with Christ is to walk by sight. The disembodied soul, therefore, has ceased to walk by faith and sees God face-to-face.

Hence, St. Paul could write, "Christ shall be magnified in my body, whether it be by life or by death, for to me, to live is Christ and to die is gain. And if to live in the flesh, this is to me the fruit of labor; and what I shall choose I know not. But I am straitened between two: having a desire to be dissolved and to be with Christ, a thing by far the better. But to abide still in the flesh is needful for you."[61] St. Paul did not know what to desire, whether to die and be with Christ or to remain on earth, where he was so much needed by the infant Church. Clearly he expected immediate heavenly bliss after death.

The same thought is embodied in those famous words, which it were well that we might all make our own when

---

[61] Phil. 1:20-24.

the course of life is over: "The time of my dissolution is at hand. I have fought a good fight; I have finished my course; I have kept the faith. As to the rest, there is laid up for me a crown of justice, which the Lord, the just Judge, will render to me in that day; and not only to me, but to them also that love His coming."[62]

[62] 2 Tim. 4:6-8.

Appendix

⸎

Are there seven heavens?

A question has been raised regarding the plurality of heavens, which at first sight seems indicated in some texts of Scripture.

Christ is said to have ascended above all heavens.[63] He has passed through the heavens and been "made higher than the heavens."

St. Paul was taken up to the third Heaven.[64]

Christ and the faithful are to be together "in the superheavens," for such is the real meaning of the Greek word *epourania* in Ephesians.[65]

[63] Eph. 4:10; Heb. 7:26.
[64] 2 Cor. 12:2.
[65] Eph. 1:3, 20; 2:6; 3:10; 6:12.

In the Old Testament, God dwells in the heaven of heavens.[66]

In medieval times, the theory of the three heavens was commonly accepted. These heavens were called either the aerial, the sidereal, and the empyrean, or the sidereal, the crystalline, and the empyrean.

According to the first theory, the first heaven is the air in which the birds and the clouds move; the second is the firmament of the stars; the third is the Heaven in which God and the blessed dwell.

According to the second theory, the starry sky, or sidereal heaven, is the lowest; upon this follows the crystalline — that is, the blue transparent dome, apparently beyond the stars; and finally the empyrean, or "fiery," Heaven of God and the angels.

Neither of these explanations of the term *third heaven* can be traced to the first century, and they give the impression of being suggested by the text of St. Paul rather than to be genuine explanations of it. St. Thomas and the Scholastics suggested purely philosophical explanations of the third heaven. It might be an intellectual vision, as

[66] Deut. 10:14; 3 Kings 8:27 (RSV = 1 Kings 8:27); Ps. 148:4.

distinguished from a mere corporeal or even an imaginative one. It might be a knowledge of God Himself, as distinguished from the knowledge of celestial bodies or celestial spirits. It might be a vision equal to that of the third and highest hierarchy of angels. These speculations, however, have no root in tradition or history.

Some of the very early Fathers imagined that the sevenfold division of the heavens was a fact and by implication taught in Holy Scripture. The idea of seven heavens is certainly one that goes back to extreme antiquity. It probably arose in early Babylonian or even Sumerian times and was connected with the sun, the moon, and the five planets then known. This purely material conception of seven concentric revolving spheres developed apparently in Jewish circles of our Lord's time into a sevenfold abode of spirits and superterrestrial beings. The third heaven is not always described in the same way in Jewish literature; it was certainly sometimes described as Paradise or the Garden of Eden.

It is remarkable that St. Paul, having spoken of the third heaven, immediately afterward refers to the same place as Paradise. It must be remembered also that our Lord Himself used the term *Paradise* for the unconsummated bliss promised to the penitent thief on the Cross. It seems most likely, therefore, that St. Paul makes use of a current expression without necessarily endorsing contemporary Jewish fancies, out of which the use of the word had grown; in the same way as we speak of being "in the seventh heaven" without in any sense thereby expressing approval of any theory of seven heavens.

The *third heaven* and *Paradise* were simply terms commonly understood of a state and place of bliss bestowed by God on the just after death. Our Lord on the Cross used toward the common brigand by His side a word that he would readily understand.

So likewise St. Paul, in speaking of a third heaven, may have used a phrase intelligible to those whom he addressed, without in any way endorsing the theory of seven or of any other number of heavens. The question whether St. Paul on that occasion received a momentary glimpse or some approximation to the Beatific Vision has been variously answered and cannot be settled through lack of information. It is, however, more commonly held that the Beatific Vision as such is withheld from those who are sojourners on earth.

৵

J. P Arendzen

(1873-1954)

John Peter Arendzen studied with the Christian Brothers
in his native Amsterdam and later at Hageveld College in
Leyden, at St. Thomas's Seminary in Hammersmith, London, at the Universities of Bonn and Munich, and at
Christ's College in Cambridge, England. He was ordained
a priest in 1895.

During his studies at Cambridge, he was assigned to St.
Ives parish as a member of the Catholic Missionary Soci-
ety, founded by Cardinal Vaughan in 1902. He taught at
St. Edmund's College in Ware until 1949 and spent his remaining years in Kilburn, North London.

The eloquence and clarity that earned him a place in the
Daily Mail's "Preachers of the Century" is reflected in his
writings, which include books, such as *Prophets, Priests,*

and Publicans and *Purgatory and Heaven*, essays, annotations in the Douay Bible, and entries in the *Catholic Encyclopedia*. Fr. Arendzen's strong, clear explanations of the Faith challenge, equip, and motivate today's readers to continue his missionary work of spreading the gospel in our increasingly secular world.

꙳

Sophia Institute Press®

Sophia Institute® is a nonprofit institution that seeks to restore man's knowledge of eternal truth, including man's knowledge of his own nature, his relation to other persons, and his relation to God. Sophia Institute Press® serves this end in numerous ways: it publishes translations of foreign works to make them accessible to English-speaking readers; it brings out-of-print books back into print; and it publishes important new books that fulfill the ideals of Sophia Institute®.

These books afford readers a rich source of the enduring wisdom of mankind. Sophia Institute Press® makes these high-quality books available to the public by using advanced technology and by soliciting donations to subsidize its publishing costs. Your generosity can help Sophia Institute Press® to provide the public with editions of works containing the enduring wisdom of the ages. Please send your tax-deductible contribution to the address below. We also welcome your questions, comments, and suggestions.

For your free catalog, call:
Toll-free: 1-800-888-9344

or write:
Sophia Institute Press®
Box 5284
Manchester, NH 03108

or visit our website:
www.sophiainstitute.com